My Songs

Cody James Votaw
My Songs

Published by Spines
ISBN: 979-8-89691-235-4

My Songs

Cody James Votaw

Contents

1

Beyond The River

I'm, above all, who stand

I'm above those who leak before me

Feel no pain, no blood

Feel last in life

Above you all

I'm beyond the river

I'm above those who kill, give and take

I see men die before I above you all.

I'm beyond the River

I'm I sain?

Am I broken?

Am I black inside?

Feel no pain, no blood, feel lost in this life. I am, above all, who stand

I'm Beyond the river

Where do I stand? Am I gone?

Where do I stand? Am I gone?

Feel but lost in a pray.

I'm above those who lie before me

I'm beyond the river

Am I sain?

Am I broken?

Am I black inside?

2

Fear Of Voices

Time kills all scars.

Time kills you

Runaway

I could kill you

But don't

Hide from corporate blood

Slow Burn kills the taste

Laughing out loud

Nine days you die

Lies in my head

Sacrifice the day

For my shit

I could kill you

But live a life of pain

And sadness

Now, I've gone wrong

Time can kill my scars

Don't worry

I'll never leave

Help me

Can't help myself

Help me

(Guitar solo)

Bodied burned

Help me get back

Love and fear

Kills my sanity

I can't change

Now, I've gone wrong

Help me

Can't help myself

Help me

Can't help myself

Time kills all scars.

Runway, I could kill you.

But stay in hell

3

River Of Doom

Hell on earth

see what I want to see

Hear what I want to hear

Pervert my sins

Mistreat those who kill thee

Have I treatment of your shit

Sick and Twisted

It's Stays with me

Down my body in the water

Kill me so I can't live anymore

Scar my body

With your burned hands

Free all my sins

Sinking lower

Down my sins

Suffer my fate

Let go of the past

It's killing swiftly

Feed the mouth full of hate

Before you go to sleep

No things said will die.

Sinking lower

Down my sins

Suffer my fate

Kill my self in this river.

Burn my soul

With all it takes

All I see is my death

See my friend dying

Never seen him

Decomposing

Sinking lower

Down my sins

Suffer my fate

4

Too Late

If this it

If it's over

Tell me now

Can't keep on this love

365 days 7 days a week

If it's over, don't leave me here to wonder

If it's too late, if it's too late for love

Please tell me so

If it's too late, if it's too late for love

Please tell me so

Day and night, I play the fool

Waiting for you

prayed every day and night

That you would come back to me

If it's too late if it's too late for love

Please tell me so

Do I say goodbye?

Do I leave it alone?

Will I stay and keep hanging on

If it's too late, if it's too late for love

Please tell me so

5

End Of The Hour About Covid 19

In a day, our House falls apart

In an hour, everything has changed

So I'll stand by you till it ends

So I'll stand until the end of the hour

Blink of an eye

You lose it all

Horror of your

Affair steps in

So I'll stand by you till it ends

So I'll stand until the end of the hour

What will you do when world stops

Will you stand up and fight

Or let it pass you by

So I'll stand by you till it ends

So I'll stand until the end of the hour

6

Can't Fool My Heart

Here I've been before

Falling in your love

Again

Thinking About You

And the things we said

And the way I treated you

But this time, you can't fool my heart

Again

Never (x2) again

The phone rings this morning
and I hear you call my name
Time and time again
I fall like a fool for you

But now, baby, you can't fool me
Again
Never (x2) again

Our love was a lie
Only thinking about our selfs
And our desires

But now, baby, you can't fool my...
Again
Never again

7

Dark September About a Drug Breakdown

Not alright today

Blood on the floor

Look my self

Blame my self

Point the finger at me

In my mind still the same

In this dark September

Get born than die

Lay down the law

I Laugh you off

Prone to feel pain

Still, I'm sane?

In my mind still the same

In this dark September

Get born than die

Day gone

Wasted to loss of life

Loss of life again

In my mind still the same

In this dark September

Get born than die

8

Oprør

Hands in ichor

Turn to watch this Death go by

Pure intention

Disturbance with

In your self

Look the other way

To these Wrongs

Libration enters conscious

Descending through its path

intolerance

Fear enters your darkness.

Tackling its inner rage

And selfish plan

Libration enters conscious

Descending through its path

intolerance

Slipping into a cold world

thoughts like a bomb

Shattered, ready to erupt

Libration enters conscious

Descending through its path

Intolerance

9

Rolling Heads

Tied up

Death on my mind

Suicide rolling loud

In my head

Everything torn

For sacrifice

Sit and watch me bleed

Sit and watch me feed

Your shit

Victim of domestic

Slayed

By my rolling heads

My Nightmare

That never ends

Wake up

On a leash

Come and die

Come and go

Come and die

Victim of domestic

Slayed

By my rolling heads

Victim of domestic

Slayed

By my rolling heads

10

Acid Rain

Water rising

Body's dead all over

Free the souls from this world

Breaking you to peace

Broken and worry

Lost In the acid rain

Can't let go

Can't hold on

Rarely see me cry;

send your soul to heaven

Wonder if it's my guilt

Killing me

Broken and worry

Lost in this acid rain

Can't let go

Can't hold on

Yea

(Solo)

Country heading for war

Lord, what am I fighting for? Victory not worth my sorrow

Life burned to this acid rain

Broken and worry

Lost in the acid rain

Can't let go

Can't hold on

11

Lonesome Cowboy

Oh, I'm a lonesome cowboy

Long, long way from home

I'm just that lonesome cowboy

Long, long way from home

ain't been the same since my baby's been gone

Well, I been outside of Texas

Into Louisiana

Even been down Clark's dale

Seen that pretty river

Sill I'm a lonesome cowboy

Since my baby's been gone

I'm a lonesome cowboy

Since my baby's been gone

She kicked me out of the house

Not letting me stay around

She said Baby, you don't

Make no money

To pay for all these bills

And stay out

Until sunrise

Can't take care of me

Can't take care of yourself

I'm still a lonesome cowboy

A long Waw from home

Oh, I'm still a lonesome cowboy

A long way from home

12

Can't Fool My Heart

Here I've been before

Falling in your love

Again

Thinking About You

And the things we said

And the way I treated you

But this time, you can't fool my heart

Again

Never (x2) again

The phone rings this morning

and I hear you call my name

Time and time again

I fall like a fool for you

But now, baby, you can't fool my

Again

Never (x2) again

Our love was a lie

Only thinking about our selfs

And our desires

But now, baby, you can't fool my

Again

Never again

13

Cold Day in Hell

Innocence

Gone astray

Life turned like a cold winter morning. Can't escape the sufferings of Your life

Hell, a short mile away

Can't escape the cold

Can't leave this well

Cold day in hell

For In this house is only hate and death.

I ask for my soul to keep

When I take this breath

Hell, a short mile away

Can't escape the cold

Can't leave this hell

Cold day in hell

Hollow be thyme name

Devil, take my soul

Same mistake

Can't go back again

Can't go back Again

Can't be saved

Can't be healed

Help me die

Can't live anymore

Help me die. I can't live anymore

Help me die. I can't live anymore

Help me die

14

Soul Asylum

Evil eyes stair before me

Shadows stand tall behind

Soul too out of reach to be save

Fork in the road

Stuck in my soul asylum

Been here before

All the same shit to me

Can't live in the past

Can't look to the future

Fork in the road

Stuck in my soul asylum

Sweating beating on walls all around me

Here I've been before, still the same shit to me

Fork In The Road

Stuck in my soul asylum

Here lays part of me

Dead on the ground

Here lays part of the Dead on the ground

Here lays part of me

Dead on the ground

Here lies part of me!!!!

Fork in the road

Stuck in this fucking soul asylum

15

American Made

It's deep in my heart.

Deep in my soul

It's with me

Never leaves me wherever I go

Oh, through and through

I'm American Made

My love is pure

My love is true

It doesn't matter what

Group you're in

Because oh

Your American made

Protect what's yours.

Protect what's mine

Protect all the freedoms

That makes us free

Home of the free was

Never free

And you can never take that away from me

Because, oh, we're American-made

Oh, we're American-made

Can't take these things away

Oh, because I'm American-made

16

Heavens Here Somewhere

She never said goodbye to me.

She was gone as quickly as she came

Said some things we both regret

Said something we wish we could

Take back

Lord, I am a sinner

I ain't perfect

But one thing I know

Heavens here somewhere

Can't mend this heart of mine

Since she's been gone

Beer, whiskey, wine kill this pain away

Lord, I am a sinner

I ain't perfect

But one thing I know

Heavens here somewhere

Woke last night, still you were gone

These Dreams can't destroy these memories I have for you

Lord, I am a sinner

I ain't perfect

But one thing I know

Heavens here someone

17

Can't Fool My Heart

Here I've been before

Falling in your love

Again

Thinking About You

And the things we said

And the way I treated you

But this time, you can't fool my heart

Again

Never (x2) again

The phone rings this morning

and I hear you call my name

Time and time again

I fall like a fool for you

But now, baby, you can't fool me

Again

Never (x2) again

Our love was a lie

Only thinking about our selfs

And our desires

But now, baby, you can't fool my...

Again

Never again

18

Third Eye

Can't believe what's come before me

Fears tower over my head

With Suicide

Rolling Heads watch over me

With ill intent

Used and abused

For gain

Broken to dust

Free from pain

Defamed

Controlled

Mind

Used for gain

To use To be

Crawling on eggshells

Used and abused for gain

Broken to dust

Free from pain

All eyes stare with loneliness.

Distance

Pave this road

Hard to do

Used and abused for gain

Broken to dust-free

From pain

www.ingramcontent.com/pod-product-compliance
Lightning Source LLC
LaVergne TN
LVHW020526160826
845677LV00015B/3920
* 9 7 9 8 8 9 6 9 1 2 3 5 4 *